Clothes

Ruth Thomson

Watts Books
London • New York • Sydney

Note for parents and teachers

The Changing Times series is soundly based on the requirements of the new History Curriculum. Using the device of four generations of a real family, the author combines reminiscences of this family with other people's oral evidence. The oral history is matched with photographs and other contemporary sources. Many other lessons are hidden in the text, which practises the skills of chronological sequencing, gives reference to a timeline and introduces the language and vocabulary of the past. Young children will find much useful information here, as well as a new understanding of the recent history of everyday situations and familiar things.

© Watts Books 1992

Paperback edition 1995

Watts Books
96 Leonard Street
London
EC2A 4RH

Franklin Watts Australia
14 Mars Road
Lane Cove
NSW 2066

UK ISBN: 0 7496 0872 2 (hardback)
UK ISBN: 0 7496 1801 9 (paperback)

Dewey Decimal Classification Number 391

A CIP catalogue record for this book is available from the British Library.

Editor: Sarah Ridley
Designer: Michael Leaman
Educational consultant: John West
Picture researcher: Sarah Moule

Acknowledgements: The publishers would like to thank the following people and organisations for their help with the preparation of this book: Anthea Jarvis of The Gallery of English Costume, Manchester; the Pearce family; the Methodist Homes for the Aged; Kim Sinclair of Kitchen and Country Antiques, Diana Green, and Peter and Alison Walton for the loan of objects from their collections.

Printed in Malaysia

Contents

These are the clothes that I like to wear – tracksuits, t-shirts and trainers.

For school, I wear school uniform.

4

My friends are wearing their favourite clothes too – jeans, blouses and skirts, sweatshirts and trousers, tracksuits and jumpers.

PUBLIC FOOTPATH TO GREAT BRINGTON

Mum washes most of my clothes in a washing machine at home.

They are often dried in the tumble-dryer.

Washing liquid and powder

On fine days, we hang
the washing outside to dry.

Some of my friends' mums
take their clothes
to a launderette.

Dad now

Dad aged six in 1965

2000   1975   1950

I asked Mum and Dad what sort of clothes
children wore when they were young.

Dad said,

'For school,
I wore shorts,
even in winter.
I didn't wear
long trousers
until I went to
senior school.'

'For every day, I wore shorts or
trousers with a shirt in summer,
and a jumper in winter.'

CHUM SHOES

Chum's Shoes
A Fitting Friend
for the Boy's Feet

'My shoes were leather lace-ups.
I had to polish them a lot.'

Mum said,

'In summer, we wore
short cotton dresses,
or shorts and t-shirts.'

'In winter, we wore kilts
or skirts with pleats
and a cardigan. Mum knitted
most of my cardigans herself.'

'When we were older, we wore
flared jeans and a stripey jumper.'

9

I asked Mum and Dad
what they wore outdoors.

Mum said,

'In the winter, I wore a grey coat
and a beret for school.'

'In the summer, everyone
wore blazers.'

'When I was a teenager,
I had a trouser suit.
I loved the
matching jacket
and trousers.'

Dad said,

'I had a long navy coat with a belt.'

'I wore
a blazer,
shorts
and a cap
to school.'

'When I was older, I had a duffle coat.
Lots of boys and girls wore those.'

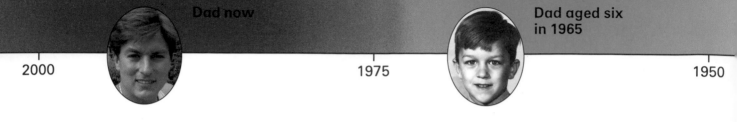
I wanted to know what Mum and Dad wore for best.

Dad said,

'I wore a white shirt,
a suit and a tie.'

Mum said,

'I never went to a party
without a party dress
and white socks.'

I asked Mum how her clothes were washed.

She said,

'We had a washing machine. It was very noisy.'

Washing powder

'Lots of our clothes were made of nylon or crimplene.
My mum liked them because they didn't need ironing.'

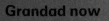
I asked my grandad and granny
what they wore when they were young.

Grandad said,

'We never chose our own clothes.
We had what was bought or made
for us and that was that.'

'We wore shorts
just above the knee,
long grey socks, shirts
and jackets.'

WELDON
SERIES No. 360.
1 TO 10
YEARS
BOYS' WEAR
6ᵈ
FREE – ALL these Patterns inside

14

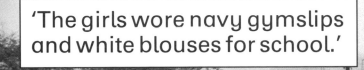

'The girls wore navy gymslips and white blouses for school.'

'On Sundays, we wore our best clothes. Cotton dresses for the girls and shorts and shirts for the boys.'

Granny said,

'My mother made
most of my dresses.
I wanted dresses
and curls like Shirley Temple's.
She was a child film star.'

'My mother put rags in my hair
at night to make it curl.'

Shirley Temple

'In the papers,
we often saw pictures
of the royal children.
Lots of people copied
the way that they looked.'

Queen Elizabeth and
Princess Margaret
when they were young.

16

I asked Grandad how his clothes were washed.

He said,

'We washed our clothes by hand. There were washing machines but we didn't have one.'

'My mum used a mangle to wring out the clothes before hanging the washing out to dry.'

Grandad said,

'During the war against Germany, clothes factories made soldiers' uniforms. People couldn't buy all the clothes they wanted.'

'Everyone had a ration book with coupons.'

'We had to hand over some of our coupons when we bought clothes.'

'My mother went to Make-do and Mend classes. She learned how to use the material from old clothes to make new ones.'

Go through your wardrobe

Make-do and Mend

'Because clothes were so scarce, we went to a Clothes Exchange to swop our outgrown coats and shoes for the next size up.'

I asked my great-granny if her clothes
were anything like mine. She laughed and said,

'My clothes were quite different from yours.
They were made only of wool or cotton
and clothes didn't come in bright colours.
Children's clothes were very like adults' clothes.'

'Girls dressed as girls.
I never ever wore trousers.'

'Boys were dressed as girls
until they were three
or four years old.'

20

'I wore plain, loose dresses for school.
I had a white pinafore on top
to keep my dresses clean.'

'Boys wore a cap,
summer or winter.
They had to raise it slightly
if they met an older person
they knew in the street.'

Great-granny said,

'For Sunday best, I wore
a starched white dress with petticoat
and thick, black woollen stockings.
I always had a bow in my hair.'

Button hook

'My boots had
stiff buttons.
I always used
a button hook
to do them up.'

22

'Boys wore suits with a matching waistcoat, and a bow tie.
The shirts had little stiff, starched collars.'

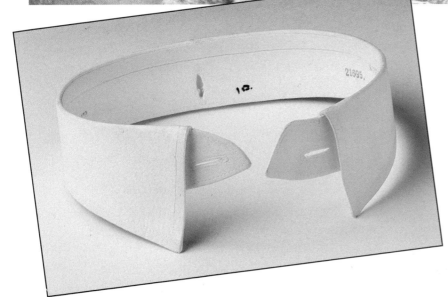

'The collars unbuttoned from the shirts so that they could be washed separately.'

Great-granny said,

'Some children didn't get many new clothes.
They wore hand-me-downs
or bought clothes from a second-hand shop.'

Darning
mushroom

'My mother was forever
sewing on buttons and mending
and patching our clothes.
She knitted all our woollens
and darned the holes in our socks.'

'Shoes were very expensive.
Some people took their worn shoes to the cobbler to mend.'

Last

'Father mended ours at home on a metal foot, called a last.'

'Sometimes shoes had metal studs put on the soles to make them last longer.'

Pair of clogs

25

Great-granny remembered how clothes were washed when she was young.

She said,

'Washing was usually done on Mondays. It took all day and was hard work.'

Posser

'The clothes were soaked in hot, soapy water in a dolly tub. Then they were swished about with a posser or a dolly stick.'

'Stains were scrubbed hard on a washboard, using a brush and soap.'

'When all the clothes were washed, my mother emptied the tub and filled it with clean water for rinsing. It was a messy business.'

'The wet clothes were put through a mangle.
Two big rollers squeezed the water out.'

'Everything was hung outside to dry.
Strong wooden pegs held the heavy clothes on the line.'

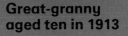

'On wet days the washing was hung
on a rail, in front of the fire.'

Flat iron

'The clothes were ironed
with heavy flat irons.
One iron was heated on the fire
while the other was being used.'

Things to do

Find out what sort of underwear
people used to wear.
Show them these pictures.

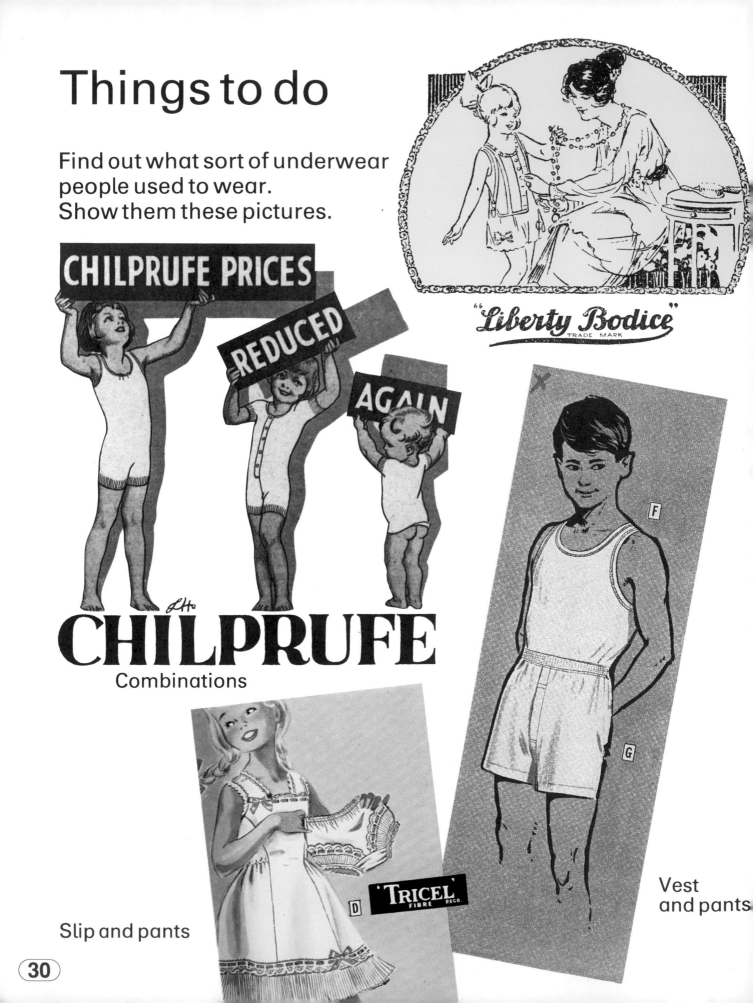

"Liberty Bodice" TRADE MARK

CHILPRUFE PRICES

REDUCED

AGAIN

CHILPRUFE
Combinations

'TRICEL' FIBRE REGO.

Slip and pants

Vest
and pants

Fashions change.

You can often tell when a photo was taken by the clothes people are wearing.

Can you put these pictures in order?
Which is the oldest?
Look back through the book to help you.

Index

Photographs: thanks to Mrs Jessie Baker cover(tr), title page(l), 15(b); Beamish 14(b), 15(t), 25(tl), 26(tl), 26(br), 28(r); Camera Press 8(t), 8(bl), 11(tl); Mary Evans Picture Library 16(t), 30(tr); Eye Ubiquitous cover(br); Chris Fairclough Colour Library title page(r), 4(t), 4(b), 5(t), 5(br), 7(t); Format 5(bl), 7(b); Francis Frith Collection 20; Sally and Richard Greenhill 6(t); Robert Harding Picture Library cover(bl), 9(t), 9(br), 13(b); Hulton Picture Company 17(t), 17(b), 18(b), 21(both), 24(t), 31(tr);

thanks to the Trustees of the Imperial War Museum 19(all); Lever Brothers 6(br); thanks to Littlewoods 30(br), 30(bl); Billie Love Collection 23(t); Peter Millard imprint page, 9(bl), 18(t), 22(r), 23(b), 24(b), 25(tr), 25(b), 26(tr), 27(r), 29(b); Robert Opie 13(tl), 14(t); Proctor and Gamble Ltd 6(bl); thanks to Mrs Jessie Ridley 10(t), 10(c), 31(c), 31(br); Topham 10(b), 11(r), 11(bl), 12(t), 12(b), 13(tr), 27(t); Unilever plc 28(l); Welsh Folk Museum 29(t).